Editors
Jennifer Overend Prior, M. Ed.
Gisela Lee

Editorial Manager
Karen J. Goldfluss, M.S. Ed.

Editor-in-Chief
Sharon Coan, M.S. Ed.

Cover Artist
Jessica Orlando

Art Coordinator
Denice Adorno

Creative Director
Elayne Roberts

Imaging
Alfred Lau
James Edward Grace

Product Manager
Phil Garcia

Publisher
Mary D. Smith, M.S. Ed.

How to Succeed in
Pre-Algebra

Grades 5–8

Auth

Charles

Teacher Created Resources, Inc.
6421 Industry Way
Westminster, CA 92683
www.teachercreated.com
ISBN-1-57690-959-X

Teacher Created Resources

Table of Contents

A Note to Teachers and Parents

Welcome to the "How to" math series! You have chosen one of over two dozen books designed to give your children the information and practice they need to acquire important concepts in specific areas of math. The goal of the "How to" math books is to give children an extra boost as they work toward mastery of the math skills established by the National Council of Teachers of Mathematics (NCTM) as outlined in grade-level scope and sequence guidelines.

The design of this book is intended to allow it to be used by teachers or parents for a variety of purposes and needs. Each of the units contains one or more "How to" pages and one or more practice pages. The "How to" section of each unit precedes the practice pages and provides needed information such as a concept or math rule review, important terms and formulas to remember, and/or step-by-step guidelines necessary for using the practice pages. While most "How to" pages are written for direct use by the children, in some lower-grade-level books, these pages are presented as instructional pages or direct lessons to be used by a teacher or parent prior to introducing the practice pages.

About This Book

The activities in this book will help your children learn new skills or reinforce skills already learned in the following areas:

- developing concepts of positive and negative numbers
- developing an understanding of algebraic expressions
- developing an understanding of algebraic equations
- learning to solve equations with one and two variables
- learning to graph solutions to one- and two-variable equations

Algebra has practical, real-life applications in architecture, product design, engineering, and graphic design. With these concepts in hand, children are prepared for the next step: drafting using software such as CAD-CAM and other practical arts.

How to Succeed in Pre-Algebra: Grades 5–8 presents a comprehensive, step-by-step overview of these fundamental mathematical concepts with clear, simple, instructional activities. The 12 units in this book can be used in whole-class instruction by a teacher or by a parent assisting his or her child with the concepts and exercises.

This book also lends itself to use by small groups doing remedial or review work in algebra or by children and small groups in earlier grades engaged in enrichment or advanced work. Finally, this book can be used in a learning center with materials specified for each unit of instruction.

If children have difficulty with a specific concept or unit in this book, review the material and allow them to redo pages that are difficult for them. Since step-by-step concept development is essential, it's best not to skip sections of the book. Even if children find a unit easy, mastering the problems will build their confidence as they approach more difficult concepts.

This book is designed to match the standards of the National Council of Teachers of Mathematics. The standards strongly support the learning of isolating variables and graphing and other basic processes in the context of problem solving and real-world applications. Use every opportunity to have students apply these new skills in classroom situations and at home. This will reinforce the value of the skills as well as the process. This book matches a number of NCTM standards including these main topics and specific features.

Concepts of Positive and Negative Numbers

Positive and negative numbers take students into a realm of mathematics they may not have visited before. Accustomed as they are to addition and subtraction, however, it is a small but necessary step into thinking about "less than zero."

Concepts of Algebraic Expressions

Variables open a door to intriguing possibilities about solving for the unknown quantity. Word problems, often so difficult for students to frame as problems, tend to contain variables. Understanding the nature of algebraic expressions is a big step toward setting up word problems.

Concepts of Algebraic Equations

Students already involved in fundamental chemistry will see an immediate connection between algebraic equations and conducting experiments to uncover unknown amounts and temperatures. Likewise, students who have a fundamental grasp of geometry will see familiar formulas in a new light as algebraic equations, not just recipes.

Solving Equations with One and Two Variables

This book provides step-by-step instructions about isolating variables to find their values. Once students understand the routine of performing an inverse operation, the rest is easy.

Graphing Solutions to One- and Two-Variable Equations

Students who are visual learners will find that showing the solutions to equations as graphs is satisfyingly concrete. Also, students who have an interest in mechanical arts will see the fundamentals of engineering unfold as they learn to show lines as mathematical shapes.

Other Standards

This book aligns well with other standards which focus on teaching computational skills—addition, subtraction, multiplication, and division—within the context of algebra.

1 ► How to ············ Add and Subtract Positive and Negative Numbers

Facts to Know

As you know, in mathematics, the plus sign (+) means add and the minus sign (–) means subtract. In algebra, there are plus and minus signs, too. Positive and negative numbers are called *signed numbers*.

Writing and Ordering Positive and Negative Numbers

Numbers can be shown on a *number line*. Numbers to the right of zero are *positive*. (The + sign won't be used in front of positive numbers in this book.) Numbers to the left of zero are *negative*.

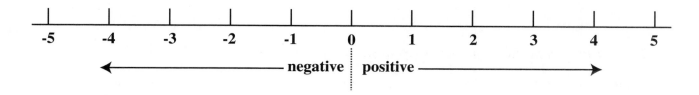

You count to the right if there is a gain in amount. You count to the left if there is a loss. Zero is neither positive nor negative.

For any two numbers on a number line, the number to the right is always greater. The symbol > means "greater than." For any two numbers on a number line, the number to the left is always less. The symbol < means "less than."

Because -3 is to the left of -1, we say -3 < -1. But 4 is to the right of 1 so we say 4 > 1.

A thermometer is an vertical number line.

For any two numbers, the higher number on the line is greater.

For instance, 10° above zero is greater than (>) -5° below zero.

Adding Positive and Negative Numbers

When adding positive and negative numbers, keep three rules in mind.

Rule 1: *The sum of two positive numbers is positive.* You simply add the numbers and get a larger positive number.

$$2 + 3 = 5$$

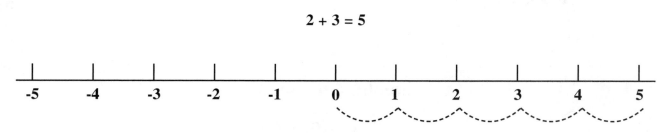

Facts to Know *(cont.)*

Rule 2: *The sum of two negative numbers is negative.* Simply add the numbers and place a minus sign in front of the answer. Parentheses make a problem easier to read. The sign goes with the number inside the parentheses.

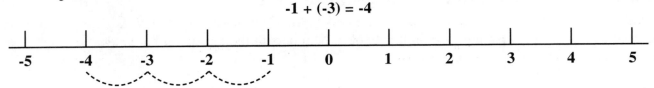

$$-1 + (-3) = -4$$

Rule 3: *The sum of a positive and negative number may be any one of the following:*

- **Zero**

    $4.5 + (-4.5) = 0$

- **Positive**

    Find the difference between the two numbers and use the sign of the larger number.

    $7 + (-2) = 5$ (Because 7 is larger than 2 and positive, the answer is also positive.)

- **Negative**

    Find the difference between the two numbers and use the sign of the larger.

    $-8 + 3 = -5$ (Because 8 is larger than 3 and negative, the answer is also negative.)

Adding More Than Two Numbers

To add more than two numbers at a time that have different signs, add the positive numbers, add the negative numbers, and then combine the sums.

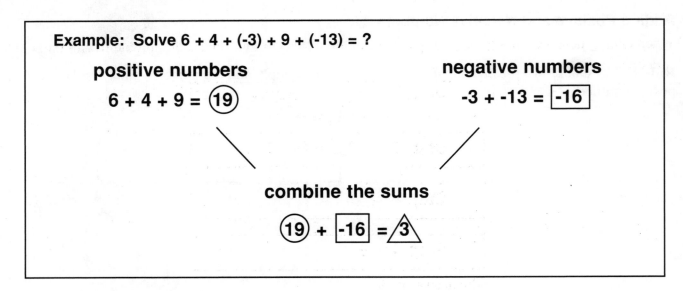

Example: Solve $6 + 4 + (-3) + 9 + (-13) = ?$

positive numbers

$6 + 4 + 9 =$ ⑲

negative numbers

$-3 + -13 =$ -16

combine the sums

⑲ + -16 = △3

Facts to Know *(cont.)*

Subtracting Positive and Negative Numbers

When subtracting signed numbers, change the sign of the number following the minus sign to its opposite and change the minus sign to plus.

$$\begin{array}{r} 4 \\ -\ \underline{-2} \end{array} \quad \xrightarrow{\textit{changes to}} \quad \begin{array}{r} 4 \\ +\ \underline{2} \end{array} \qquad \textit{The answer is 6.}$$

Think of it this way—the difference between 4 and -2 on a number line is *6 steps*.

If the problem is set up horizontally instead of vertically the sign inside the parentheses goes with the number. Change the sign of the second number and add.

$$(-1) - (-4) = \quad \xrightarrow{\textit{changes to}} \quad (-1) + (+4) = \qquad \textit{The answer is 3.}$$

Think of it this way—the difference between -1 and -4 is *3 steps*.

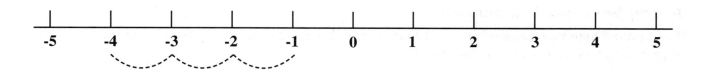

Here are the steps involved in an example of changing the signs in a subtraction problem with three numbers:

> **Step 1: (-7) – 4 – (-2) = ?**

> **Step 2: (-7) + (-4) + 2 = ?**

> **Step 3: (-11) + 2 = ?**

> **Step 4: -9**

The answer is -9.

Adding and Subtracting Positive and Negative Numbers

Directions: On each number line, write the number that X represents.

1.

2.

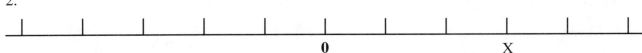

3.

Directions: Find the sum.

4.	6.	8.	10.
-3	-60	-2.3	1.3
-4	-20	-5	2.89
+ -2	+ -30	+ 10	+ 3.7

5.	7.	9.	11.
5	-12	-4	-8
2	-31	8	7
+ 2	+ 0	+ 19	-9
			+ 4

Directions: Find the difference.

12. $8 - 4 =$ _____

13. $-4 - 9 =$ _____

14. $(12) - (-3) =$ _____

15. $-9 - (-3) =$ _____

16. $9 - (-3) =$ _____

17. $-30 - (-80) =$ _____

18. $0 - (-12) =$ _____

19. $4 - 0 =$ _____

20. $9 - 2 =$ _____

21. $2 - 9 =$ _____

22. $8 - 3.6 =$ _____

23. $3.6 - 8 =$ _____

24. $7 - (-11) =$ _____

25. $-3 - (-15) =$ _____

26. $5 - (-12) =$ _____

Directions: Find the difference or sum.

27. $-7 - 4 - (-2) =$ _____

28. $5 - (-5) - (-6) =$ _____

29. $-4 - 9 - (-3) =$ _____

30. $9 - 7 - (-5) =$ _____

31. $(9 - 4) - (1 - 3) + (7 + 10) =$ _____

32. $(5 - 1) - (3 + 2) - (3 - 9) =$ _____

33. $(2 - 8) - 8 - (9 - 4) =$ _____

34. $(7 - 3) - (7 - 11) + 7 =$ _____

Facts to Know

Instead of using the symbols x or •, you can use parentheses to show multiplication. **(4)(2) = 8**
For division, you can use a line instead of a division box. $\frac{50}{2} = 25$

Multiplying Positive and Negative Numbers

When multiplying positive and negative numbers, remember these rules:

Rule 1: *The product of two positive or two negative numbers is positive:*

$$\textbf{(5)(3) = 15} \qquad\qquad \textbf{(-5)(-3) = 15}$$

Rule 2: *The product of a positive number and a negative number is negative:*

$$\textbf{(4)(-2) = -8} \qquad\qquad \textbf{(-4)(2) = -8}$$

If there are more than two numbers, it is often easiest to start on the left. Work with two numbers at a time.

Example: (-3)(4)(-2) = ?

> **Step 1:** Multiply the first two numbers. **(-3)(4)(-2)**
>
> **-12**

> **Step 2:** Multiply -12 by the next number (-2). **(-12)(-2) = 24**

Shortcuts

Here are three tips to keep in mind about multiplying positive and negative numbers:

- An *even* number of negative signs results in a *positive* product.

  (-6)(5)(3)(-2) = 180

- An *odd* number of negative signs results in a *negative* product.

  (6)(5)(-3)(2) = -180

- Simplify the expressions with parentheses first.

  (2)(-3)(10 – 6 + 2)(-2 x 3) =
  (2)(-3)(6)(-6) =
  (-6)(-36) = 216

Facts to Know *(cont.)*

Instead of the symbol ÷, you can use a line to show division. $\frac{50}{2} = 25$

Dividing Positive and Negative Numbers

When dividing positive and negative numbers, the rules are the same as for multiplying. If the signs are the *same*—two positive or two negative numbers—the answer is always positive:

Example

$\frac{-80}{-4}$ means -80 divided by -4. The signs are the same, so the answer is positive. $\frac{-80}{-4} = 20$

If the signs are *different*—one positive and one negative number—the answer is always negative.

Example

$\frac{-325}{5}$ means -325 divided by 5. The signs are *different*, so the answer is negative. $\frac{-325}{5} = -65$

There can be more than one number above or below the fraction bar. Those numbers may or may not be in parentheses.

Example: $\frac{9-5}{12-14} = ?$

Step 1: Combine the numbers above the line. $\quad\quad \frac{9-5}{12-14} = \frac{4}{12-14}$

Step 2: Combine the numbers below the dividing line. $\quad \frac{9-5}{12-14} = \frac{4}{-2}$

Step 3: Divide. $\frac{4}{-2} = -2$

Facts to Know *(cont.)*

Using More Than One Operation to Solve an Equation

You may need to use more than one operation—addition, subtraction, multiplication, and division—to solve a longer equation.

Example: $2(6 - 4) - \left[\dfrac{25}{5}\right] + 3(8 - 10) = ?$

Step 1: Combine the numbers inside the parentheses.

$$\overset{(2)}{2(6 - 4)} - \left[\frac{25}{5}\right] + \overset{(-2)}{3(8 - 10)} =$$

Step 2: Multiply.

$$\overset{4}{2(2)} - \left[\frac{25}{5}\right] + \overset{-6}{3(-2)} =$$

Step 3: Reduce (simplify) by dividing.

$$4 - \left[\frac{\overset{5}{25}}{\underset{1}{5}}\right] + (-6) =$$

Step 4: Subtract.

$$\overset{(-1)}{4 - 5} + (-6) = (-1) + (-6) = -7$$

Step 5: Add.

$$2(6 - 4) - \left[\frac{25}{5}\right] + 3(8 - 10) = -7$$

Directions: Multiply.

1. $7 \times 9 =$ _____

2. $-11 \times -6.2 =$ _____

3. $-22 \times -2.1 =$ _____

4. $-1(-20)(5) =$ _____

5. $-6(-9)(1) =$ _____

6. $-12(11)(-9 + 2) =$ _____

7. $-2(-3)(-5)(-1 + 3 - 4) =$ _____

8. $(-6)(4)(1) =$ _____

9. $(5)(-7)(2) =$ _____

10. $(5-2)(-3)(3 + 1) =$ _____

11. $(7 - 3)(-3)(-2) =$ _____

12. $(2 + 4)(6 - 3)(-5) =$ _____

Directions: Divide.

13. $-16 \div 4 =$

14. $85 \div -17 =$

15. $21 \div -7 =$

16. $\dfrac{-121}{-11} =$

17. $\dfrac{-54}{-18} =$

18. $\dfrac{-72}{-8} =$

19. $\dfrac{-90}{-30} =$

20. $\dfrac{5 - 10}{15 - 20} =$

21. $\dfrac{12 - 3}{9 - 6} =$

22. $\dfrac{-84}{-12} =$

23. $\dfrac{9 + 3}{4 - 10} =$

24. $\dfrac{8 + 7}{3 + 2} =$

Directions: Find the answers.

25. $\dfrac{-81(-3 + 6)}{9} =$

26. $\dfrac{90(2 - 5)}{-5}$

27. $6(4 + 1) - 7(5 - 4) + (3 + 2) =$

28. $-5(8 + 2) + 4(6 - 9) - \left[\dfrac{30}{10} \right] =$

29. $-2(5 - 6) + 10(6 - 7) - \left[\dfrac{25}{5} \right] =$

30. $6(1 + 2) + 2(4 + 3) + \left[\dfrac{36}{12} \right] =$

31. $\dfrac{6(5 - 3) + 2(2 - 6)}{3(9 - 3)} =$

32. $\dfrac{2(1 - 6) - 7(2 + 3)}{-9(3 - 4)} =$

33. $\dfrac{2(7 - 3) + 8(5 + 2)}{2(10 - 2)} =$

34. $\dfrac{8(-10 + 7) + 4(27 - 36)}{4(5 - 2)} =$

Facts to Know

Algebra is a branch of mathematics that uses numbers and letters that stand for numbers to solve problems. In algebra, if a number is unknown, any letter of the alphabet can be used to stand for that number. Letters are called *variables* because the values of the letters vary from one problem to another. In one problem, *x* may stand for -2. In another problem, it may stand for 43.

Writing Algebraic Expressions

An *algebraic expression* is a statement made up of numbers, variables, and signs of operation $(+, -, \div, \times)$. The phrase "a number" indicates the use of the variable.

Statement in Words	*Algebraic Expression*
a number increased by 6	$x + 6$
7 decreased by a number	$7 - y$
a number divided by 12	$\dfrac{x}{12}$
a number multiplied by 4	$4(n)$
the sum of 7 and a number, divided by 3	$\dfrac{7 + y}{3}$
the sum of 4 times a number and 2	$4x + 2$
20 divided by the sum of 5 and a number	$\dfrac{20}{5 + y}$
4 times a number minus 2 times the same number	$4x - 2x$
two-fifths of a number	$\dfrac{2}{5}x$

Combining Like Terms

Sometimes algebraic expressions can be shortened by combining like terms making them simpler to understand. An expression is made up of smaller parts called *terms*. A term can be made up of numbers, variables, or numbers and variables. In an expression, terms are separated by only plus and minus signs.

Examples: 15, *x*, *xy*, 5*xy*, $\dfrac{4x}{y}$

Facts to Know *(cont.)*

A *numerical coefficient* is any number in front of a variable in a term. If there is no number in front of a varible, the numerical coefficient is understood to be 1.

Examples: 4*a*, 5*x*, 6*xy*

↑ ↑ ↑

numerical coefficients

An *exponent* tells how many times a number has been multiplied by itself. **Examples: 4^2, $8w^3$, $10n^3$**

Terms that have all of the same variables (*xy*, 3*xy*, 5*xy*, etc.) or variables with the same exponents ($4a^2 + a^2$), are called *like* or *similar terms*. Like terms can be combined by combining the numerical coefficients.

Examples

$5b + b \longrightarrow 5b + 1b \longrightarrow (5 + 1)b \longrightarrow 6b$

$9a - 2a \longrightarrow (9 - 2)a \longrightarrow 7a$

$5n + 3r - 2n \longrightarrow (5n - 2n) + 3r \longrightarrow (5 - 2)n + 3r \longrightarrow 3n + 3r$

But an algebraic expression like $9y^2 + 2y$ cannot be combined because y^2 and 2*y* are not like terms. One has an exponent of 2 and the other has a coefficient of 2.

Evaluating Algebraic Expressions

Remember that in algebra a variable can stand for any number. However, sometimes in an algebraic expression, you are given the value of the letter. Then you must replace the variables with the numbers they represent to solve for the value of the whole expression.

Example: Find the value of $\frac{a}{b}$, when $a = 20$ and $b = 4$.

Step 1: Replace *a* with its value, 20. $\frac{20}{b}$

Step 2: Replace *b* with its value. $\frac{20}{4}$

Step 3: Complete the division problem. $\frac{20}{4} = 5$

Directions: Write the algebraic expression. If there is one variable, use x. If there are two variables, use x and y.

1. fourteen divided by a number _____

2. seven times a number _____

3. 10 less than a number _____

4. 12 more than a number _____

5. one number added to another number _____

6. a number divided by 6 _____

7. 4 times a number plus 5 times the same number _____

8. 4 times a number plus 5 times another number _____

9. 7 more than one-third of a number _____

10. 25 divided by a number _____

11. the sum of 6 and a number divided by 10 _____

12. one-half the product of 8 and a number _____

13. the sum of 5 and a number divided by 7 _____

14. the sum of 4 and a number divided by 10 _____

15. 20 decreased by 4 times a number _____

16. the sum of 20 and a number divided by 5 _____

17. The length of the gym floor is 5 feet longer than its width. Using w for the width, write an expression for the length of the room. _____

18. Three carnival tickets cost c cents. What is the cost of one? _____

Directions: Change the algebraic expressions to statements in words.

Algebraic Expression	**Statement in Words**
19. $a + b$	_____
20. $s - r$	_____
21. $4y$	_____
22. $\dfrac{8}{y}$	_____
23. $2y - 5$	_____
24. $8 + y$	_____
25. xy	_____
26. $22 - t$	_____
27. $t - 22$	_____

Directions: Combine the like terms to simplify each expression.

28. $3y + y =$ _____

29. $b + b =$ _____

30. $5r - 2r =$ _____

31. $3c - 4c =$ _____

32. $\frac{2}{3}d + 3b + d =$ _____

33. $12r^2 - 3s + r =$ _____

34. $4x - 3x + 1 =$ _____

35. $2 + 3n - 7 =$ _____

36. $9x + 2y^3 - 4y - 6x =$ _____

37. $\frac{8}{2}x - 9y - 6x + 12y =$ _____

Directions: Evaluate the following expressions. Let $r = 3$ and $t = 9$.

38. $\frac{r}{t} =$ _____

39. $rt =$ _____

40. $\frac{r}{3} + \frac{t}{3} =$ _____

41. $r + t =$ _____

42. $\frac{t}{r} =$ _____

Directions: Evaluate the following expressions. Let $a = 5$, $b = -4$, and $c = 10$.

43. $ab =$ _____

44. $b + c =$ _____

45. $\frac{c}{5} =$ _____

46. $c - 5 =$ _____

47. $\frac{b}{c} =$ _____

4 ► How to ·········· Work with More Algebraic Expressions

Facts to Know

Remember from Unit 3 that an *algebraic expression* is a statement made up of numbers, variables, and signs of operation (+, −, ÷, x). An *equation* is a number sentence. It tells about equal things. An algebraic expression is only *part* of an equation. There is no equal sign in an algebraic expression.

Expressions	Equations
$9 + 1$	$9 + 1 = 10$
$10 \div 5$	$10 \div 5 = 2$
$b + 8$	$b + 8 = 12$
$(7y)^2$	$(7y)^2 = 28$

In this unit we will move from evaluating expressions only to evaluating expressions as part of solving equations.

Using More Than One Operation to Evaluate Expressions

To evaluate an algebraic expression, sometimes you need to perform more than one operation. To solve an equation, you must follow the correct order of operations.

- Simplify expressions inside the parentheses by performing the operations needed inside the parentheses.

- Multiply or divide. (Work from left to right.)

- Add or subtract. (Work from left to right.)

Not every expression will require all of the above, but that is the order in which you must use them. Each operation, done one at a time, will rapidly simplify the expression.

> **Example:** Evaluate $\dfrac{a(b + c)}{10}$ when $b = 4$, $c = 6$, and $a = -2$.

Step 1: Replace the letters with the given number values. $\dfrac{(-2)(4 + 6)}{10}$

Step 2: Combine (add or subtract) the numbers or variables inside the parentheses. $\dfrac{(-2)(10)}{10}$

Step 3: Multiply. $(-2)(10)$ is **-20**

Step 4: Divide. $\dfrac{-20}{10} = -2$

So, $\dfrac{a(b + c)}{10} = -2$ when $b = 4$, $c = 6$, and $a = -2$

Facts to Know (cont.)

Evaluating Formulas

A *formula* shows how one amount depends on one or more other amounts.

For example, the geometry formula $d = 2r$ means the diameter of a circle is twice the length of the radius. The length of the diameter depends on the length of the radius.

Notice that a formula is an *equation,* not an *expression.* The unknown amount is written to the left of the equal sign, such as *d* for diameter. The algebraic expression, such as $2r$ in the equation $d = 2r$, is written to the right of the equal sign.

Example: Find the Fahrenheit temperature if the Celsius temperature is 40°. Celsius temperatures can be converted to Fahrenheit temperatures using this formula: $F = \frac{9}{5}C + 32$

Step 1: Replace the letters with the known number values. $\qquad F = \frac{9}{5}(40) + 32$

Step 2: Reduce (simplify) and multiply. $\qquad F = \frac{9}{5}(\overset{8}{\cancel{40}}) + 32$ $\;\underset{1}{}$

Step 3: Add. $\qquad F = 72 + 32$ so $F = 104^{\circ}$

Example: Find the Celsius temperature if the Fahrenheit temperature is 50° F. Fahrenheit temperatures can be converted to Celsius temperatures using this formula: $C = \frac{5}{9}(F - 32)$

Step 1: Replace the letters with the known number values. $\qquad C = \frac{5}{9}(50 - 32)$

Step 2: Reduce (simplify) and multiply. Then add. $\qquad C = \frac{5}{9}(\overset{2}{\cancel{18}}) = 5 \times 2 = 10^{\circ}$ $\;\underset{1}{}$

Facts to Know *(cont.)*

Solving Equations with One Inverse Operation

When you solve an equation, such as the temperature formula—or any equation—you are finding the value of a variable. You must find the value of the variable that will make both sides equal.

Rule: *Whatever you do to one side of the equation, you must do to the other side to keep the equation in balance.*

Example: $a + 2 = 10$.

The variable a plus two more is equal to 10. But how do you get a alone to figure its value? Here's how:

Step 1: In $a + 2 = 10$, subtract 2 from the left side of the equals sign.

$$a + 2 = 10$$
$$\underline{-2 \quad -2}$$

Step 2: Remember, whatever you do to one side of the equation, you must do to the other. Subtract 2 from 10, too.

$$a + 2 = 10$$
$$\underline{-2 = -2}$$
$$a = 8$$

Subtracting 2 from both sides in an addition problem is an *inverse operation*. Inverse means *opposite*. Addition and subtraction are inverse operations. Multiplication and division are inverse operations. Here is a division problem.

Example: $\dfrac{x}{4} = 40$

To solve the problem use the inverse of division, which is multiplication.

Step 1: Multiply the left side by 4 to get x by itself.

$$(4)\,\frac{x}{4} = 40$$

Step 2: What you do to the left, you must do to the right. Multiply by 4.

$$(4)\frac{x}{4} = (4)40 \text{ so } x = 160$$

Directions: Evaluate the following expressions.

Let $n = 6$, $s = 5$, $t = 2$ Let $a = -3$, $b = 4$, and $c = -2$.

1. $3n + 6s =$ _____

6. $ac - b =$ _____

2. $2ns - 3s + 10 =$ _____

7. $\dfrac{bc}{ac} =$ _____

3. $9n - 4t =$ _____

8. $4b - 2c - 3a =$ _____

4. $14(n + t) =$ _____

9. $7(c + b) =$ _____

5. $3t - (n + s) =$ _____

10. $\dfrac{3a + 2a}{a} =$ _____

Directions: Solve the equations using the formulas given. _____

11. The temperature outside is 59° F. What is it in Celsius? _____
    (Use this formula: $C = \dfrac{5}{9}(F - 32)$)

12. Your family plans to go on a short weekend vacation. Your mom wants to drive only 3 hours on back roads at 45 miles per hour. How far away can you go? (Use the formula: $d = rt$ or *distance = rate* x *time*.) _____

13. Fred Tye sells electronic equipment after school at Sparky's World. He earns $140 a week, plus 7% percent commission on all sales over $1,000. Last week, Fred sold $3,000 worth of equipment. How much did he earn? (Use this formula: earnings = salary + .07 (sales – $1000). _____

14. Mr. Marky is pacing off the perimeter (the distance around) his square property. One side is 90 feet. "Don't walk the other three sides," said his wife. "Just use the formula, $P = 4s$." "What does that mean?" said Mr. Marky. "It means," said his wife, "perimeter equals 4 times the length of any one side." What's the perimeter of Mr. Marky's property?

Directions: Solve each equation using an inverse operation.

15. $3b = -36$

19. $n - 15 = 20$

16. $y + 20 = 100$

20. $-72 = 9x$

17. $24 = a - 18$

21. $-25 = \dfrac{a}{5}$

18. $\dfrac{t}{3} = 48$

22. $60 = 42 + c$

Facts to Know

Remember from Unit 4 that to evaluate an algebraic expression, sometimes you need to perform more than one operation. Perform the operations, one at a time, in this order:

- Simplify expressions by performing the operations needed inside the parentheses.

- Multiply or divide. (Work from left to right.)

- Add or subtract. (Work from left to right.)

As you also learned in Unit 3, terms that have all of the same variables (xy, $3xy$, $-5xy$, etc.) or variables with the same exponents ($4a^2 + a^2$), are called *like* or *similar terms*. Like terms can be combined by combining the numerical coefficients. A *numerical coefficient* is any number in front of a variable.

Likewise, you combine terms to solve equations just like you do in evaluating algebraic expressions.

Solving Two- and Three-Step Equations

If more than one step must be performed to solve an equation, do addition and subtraction *before* multiplication and division.

Example: Solve $4y - 4 = -16$

Step 1: Add 4 to both sides (remember about inverse operations: what you do to one side of an equation, you must do to the other).

$$\begin{array}{r} 4y - 4 = -16 \\ +4 = +4 \\ \hline 4y = -12 \end{array}$$

Step 2: Divide by 4 on both sides.

$$\frac{\overset{1y}{\cancel{4y}}}{\cancel{4}} = \frac{\overset{-3}{\cancel{-12}}}{\cancel{4}}$$

$$y = -3$$

Example: Solve $5z + 15 = 60$

Step 1: Subtract 15 on both sides. (Remember with inverse operations, what you do to one side of an equation, you must do to the other.)

$$\begin{array}{r} 5z + 15 = 60 \\ -15 - 15 \\ \hline 5z = 45 \end{array}$$

Step 2: Divide by 5 on both sides.

$$\frac{\cancel{5}z}{\cancel{5}} = \frac{\overset{9}{\cancel{45}}}{\cancel{5}}$$

$$z = 9$$

Facts to Know (cont.)

Solving Two- and Three-Step Equations (cont.)

Example: Solve $\frac{-2}{3}s + 3 = 18$

> **Step 1:** Subtract 3 from both sides of the equation.
>
> **Step 2:** Multiply by the reciprocal of $\frac{-2}{3}$ to eliminate it and leave the s by itself.

$$\frac{-2}{3}s + 3 = 18$$
$$\underline{\quad -3 \quad -3}$$
$$\frac{-2}{3}s = 15$$

$$\left(\frac{-3}{2}\right) \frac{-2}{3}s = 15\left(\frac{-3}{2}\right) = -\frac{45}{2} \text{ or } -22\frac{1}{2}$$

Combining Variables to Solve Equations

To solve equations, combine variables when you can. Then use inverse operations.

Example: Solve $2r + 4r + 12 = 120$

> **Step 1:** Combine the variables.

$$2r + 4r + 12 = 120$$
$$\underbrace{\qquad\qquad}_{6r}$$

> **Step 2:** Subtract 12 from both sides to get $6r$ by itself.

$$6r + 12 = 120$$
$$\underline{\quad -12 = -12}$$
$$6r = 108$$

> **Step 3:** Divide both sides by 6.

$$\frac{6r}{6} = \frac{108}{6} \text{ so } r = 18$$

Example: Solve $2(y - 4) = 12$

> **Step 1:** Multiply 2 and $(y - 4)$.

$$2(y - 4) = 12 \rightarrow 2y - 8 = 12$$

> **Step 2:** Add 8 to both sides to get $2y$ by itself.

$$2y - 8 = 12$$
$$\underline{\quad +8 \quad +8}$$
$$2y = 20$$

> **Step 3:** Divide both sides by 2 to get y by itself.

$$\frac{2y}{2} = \frac{\overset{10}{20}}{2} \text{ so } y = 10$$

Facts to Know (cont.)

Solving Equations with Variables on Both Sides

If there are variables and numbers on both sides of the equal sign, you will have to get all variables on one side of the equation and all numbers on the other side.

Example: $5y - 3 = 2y + 15$

Step 1: Place all variables on one side of the equation.
Since $2y$ is smaller than $5y$, subtract it from both sides.

$$\begin{array}{r} 5y - 3 = 2y + 15 \\ \underline{- 2y \qquad - 2y} \\ 3y - 3 = 15 \end{array}$$

Step 2: Add 3 to both sides to get $3y$ by itself.

$$\begin{array}{r} 3y - \cancel{3} = 15 \\ \underline{+ \cancel{3} \quad + 3} \\ 3y = 18 \end{array}$$

Step 3: Divide by 3 on both sides to get y by itself.

$$\frac{\cancel{3}y}{\cancel{3}} = \frac{\cancel{18}}{\cancel{3}} \quad \text{so } y = 6$$

Example: Solve $3x + 23 = 10x + 2$

Step 1: Place all variables on one side of the equation.
Since $3x$ is smaller than $10x$, subtract it from both sides.

$$\begin{array}{r} 3x + 23 = 10x + 2 \\ \underline{- 3x \qquad - 3x} \\ 23 = 7x + 2 \end{array}$$

Step 2: Subtract 2 from both sides to get $7x$ by itself.

$$\begin{array}{r} 23 = 7x + 2 \\ \underline{- 2 \qquad - 2} \\ 21 = 7x \end{array}$$

Step 3: Divide both sides by 7 to get x by itself.

$$\frac{\cancel{21}}{\cancel{7}} = \frac{\cancel{7}x}{\cancel{7}} \quad \text{so } x = 3$$

Directions: Solve these two- and three-step equations.

1. $8a - 4 = 60$

2. $9z - 12 = 69$

3. $\frac{b}{3} + 4 = 16$

4. $\frac{w}{12} + 8 = 30$

5. $\frac{3}{4}c - 3 = 9$

6. $39 = 14d - 3$

Directions: Combine the variables to solve the equations.

7. $7(2 + x) = 28$

8. $8x + 2 + 2x = 32$

9. $3x - 2x - 10 = -9$

10. $6(x - 3) = 18$

11. $2(3 + x) = 7$

12. $14x - 10 - 4x = 0$

13. $x + 2x + 3x = 12$

14. $y + 3y + 2(y + 3) = 15$

Directions: Solve these equations with variables on both sides.

15. $4x = 8 + 2x$

16. $5(x - 4) = 3(x + 8)$

17. $3n - 9 = 7n + 5$

18. $7a + 15 = 4a + 37$

19. $3a + 10 = 8a$

20. $2(r - 3) = 4(r - 10)$

21. $5r + 32 = 8r + 17$

22. $6y - 2 - 9y = 4$

23. $48 - 4y = 8y - 12$

24. $28 - 2x = 5x$

25. $9w + 17 = 6w + 32$

26. $19b - 14 - 21b = -2$

Facts to Know

Whether equations have numbers and letters or just letters, the key is to get the unknown variable alone on one side of the equal sign.

Removing Parentheses Before Solving Equations

In algebra, parentheses are used to show multiplication $(4)(2) = 8$ and to simplify an expression such as $2(a + 6)$, you multiply both items inside the parentheses by 2.

$$2(a + 6) \longrightarrow 2a + 2(6) \longrightarrow 2a + 12$$

This process of removing the parentheses is an important step toward solving the equation.

Example: $2(x + 5) - x = -7$

Step 1: Multiply 2 times x and 2 times 5.

$$2(x + 5) - x = -7 \longrightarrow 2x + 2(5) - x = -7 \longrightarrow 2x + 10 - x = -7$$

Step 2: Combine like terms.

$$2x + 10 - x = -7 \longrightarrow x + 10 = -7$$

Step 3: Subtract from both sides to get x by itself.

$$\begin{array}{r} x + 10 = -7 \\ -10 \quad -10 \\ \hline x = -17 \end{array}$$

Example: $38 = 2 - 3(y - 5)$

Step 1: Multiply -3 times y and -3 times -5.

$$38 = 2 - 3(y - 5) \longrightarrow 38 = 2 - 3y - 3(-5) \longrightarrow 38 = 2 - 3y + 15$$

Step 2: Combine like terms.

$$38 = 2 - 3y + 15 \longrightarrow 38 = 17 - 3y$$

Step 3: Subtract 17 from both sides.

$$\begin{array}{r} 38 = 17 - 3y \\ -17 \quad -17 \\ \hline 21 = -3y \end{array}$$

Step 4: Divide both sides by -3.

$$\frac{\overset{-7}{\cancel{21}}}{\cancel{-3}} = \frac{\overset{1y}{\cancel{-3y}}}{\cancel{-3}} \quad \text{so } y = -7$$

Facts to Know *(cont.)*

Solving Literal Equations

Some equations have no numbers, but only variables. These equations are called *literal equations*. Solve them the same way you solve equations with numbers. You need to find the desired unknown on one side of the equal sign to discover its value.

Formulas, for example, are sometimes easier to use if the unknown value is by itself. But sometimes the way a formula is written doesn't fit the problem!

Example: How long does it take to go 160 miles at 55 miles per hour?

Problems like this usually use the formula $d = rt$ or *distance = rate x time*. But to find the time, you need to get t (time) by itself.

Step 1: Divide both sides of the formula by r to get t by itself (perform an inverse operation).

$$\frac{d}{r} = \frac{rt}{r}$$

Now instead of $d = rt$, you now have $\dfrac{d}{r} = t$.

Step 2: Replace letters with values from the problem.

$$\frac{160}{55} = t \text{ so } t = 2.91$$

It takes 2.91 hours to go 160 miles at 55 miles per hour.

Here's an example in which you have no numbers at all.

Example: Solve $ax - b = c$ for x.

Remember to do addition and subtraction before multiplication and division.

Step 1: Add b to both sides as a step toward getting x by itself.

$$\begin{array}{r} ax - b = c \\ +b \ +b \\ \hline ax = c + b \end{array}$$

Step 2: Perform another inverse operation. Divide both sides by a to get x by itself.

$$\frac{ax}{a} = \frac{c + b}{a}$$

$$x = \frac{c + b}{a}$$

Directions: Solve the following equations by removing parentheses.

1. $5(x + 2) = 25$	7. $2x = 7 + 3(2 - x)$
2. $5(x + 3) = 6(x - 4)$	8. $-5(1 + x) = 8 - 4x$
3. $7(b + 2) = 28$	9. $2(4x + 11) = -3 + 3x$
4. $2(x + 3) - 4 = 8 + 6x$	10. $-7 - (-3 - 2x) = 10$
5. $4x + 3(x + 7) = 14$	11. $\frac{1}{2}(11x - 60) - 2x = x$
6. $3(2 + x) = -10 + 2x$	12. $4(x - 2) = 72$

Directions: Solve the following literal equations for the indicated variable.

1. $c + d + y = b$ Solve for y. _____

2. $tx = a + b$ Solve for x. _____

3. $sm + w = p$ Solve for m. _____

4. $x - t = r$ Solve for x. _____

5. $\frac{x}{b} = a$ Solve for x. _____

6. $x + y = w$ Solve for x. _____

7. $dx = b$ Solve for x. _____

8. $x + b = p$ Solve for x. _____

9. $h = wx$ Solve for x. _____

10. $cy = d - a$ Solve for y. _____

11. $A = lw$ Solve for l. _____

12. $d = rt$ Solve for t. _____

13. $bx + y = z$ Solve for x. _____

14. $cr + s = t$ Solve for r. _____

15. $\frac{ab}{c} = d$ Solve for b. _____

16. $\frac{rs}{t} = v$ Solve for s. _____

17. $w = x + yz$ Solve for z. _____

18. $c^2 = a^2 + b^2$ Solve for b. _____

---

19. The formula for finding the circumference of a circle with radius r is $C = 2\pi r$. Find the value of r ($\pi = 3.14$).	20. The formula for finding the perimeter of a rectangle with length l and width w is $P = 2l + 2w$. Find the value of w.

Facts to Know

A *graph* is an illustration of an equation. A graph is made up of two number lines that cross (more about this below). A graph shows the relationship of the terms in the equation. The graphs of some equations are straight lines. These are *linear equations*. The graphs of other equations can be curves or other shapes. These are called *nonlinear equations*. Can you tell the difference just by looking at an equation? Yes.

A linear equation contains one or two variables, each to the first power

Examples:	$y = 3b + 5$	$n = 4$	$t = \dfrac{1}{2}y - 8$

On the other hand, if a variable in an equation is raised to a power other than 0 or 1 —and that includes negative numbers, too—its graph will be nonlinear.

Examples: $20 = r^2$ *r is a variable raised to the second power.*
$t = \dfrac{3}{x} + 9$ *$t = \dfrac{3}{x} + 9$ is the same as $y = 3x^{-1} + 9$, raising x to the -1 power.*

Graphs are often used in engineering and other sciences to show a mathematical statement as a visual piece of information. A shape can be expressed as an equation or as a graph.

Number Lines on Graphs

A graph is made up of two number lines that intersect (cross) at right angles. One number line is *horizontal*. It is called the *x–axis*.

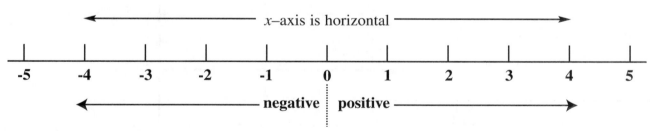

The numbers to the *right* of 0 are positive. The numbers to the *left* of 0 are negative.

Facts to Know *(cont.)*

The vertical number line is called the *y–axis*.

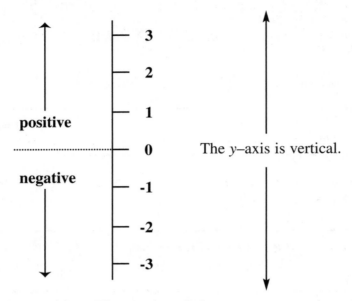

The *y*–axis is vertical.

The numbers *above* zero are positive. The numbers *below* zero are negative.

On a graph, the *x*–axis and *y*–axis cross at 0. The zero is called the *origin*. All other points are counted from zero.

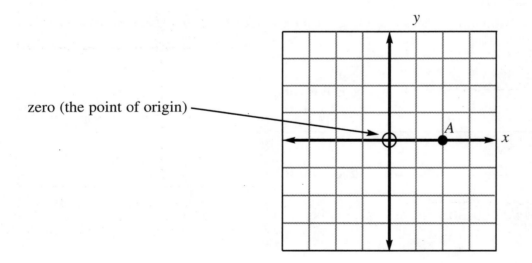

zero (the point of origin)

Points on a graph are often named by letters: *A, B, C, D* and so on. To find out what number a point stands for, count the number of lines from 0. What does the *A* stand on the graph above?

A is on the *x*–axis, two places to the right of zero. So, point *A* is at 2 on the *x*–axis. Point *A* is (2, 0).

Facts to Know *(cont.)*

Finding Coordinates for Points

Two numbers are needed to give the location of a point on a graph. The two numbers are the point's *coordinates*. Think of when you use the number scale and letter scale on the sides of a map. A town or landmark may be located at (A, 7), for instance. These are the place's coordinates.

In algebra, the coordinates are always written inside parentheses, like this:

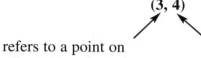

(3, 4)

- refers to a point on the *x*–axis
- refers to a point on the *y*–axis

- tells how far to the *right* or *left* of 0 the point is located
- tells how far *above* or *below* 0 the point is located

Find the coordinates for points *A* and *B* on the graph below.

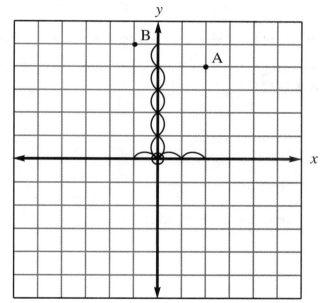

For Finding Point A

Step 1: Find the *x*–coordinate. Start at 0 and count over right to the line point *A* is on. Point *A* is 2 lines to the right of *0*. So, point *A* is has an *x*-coordinate of 2.

Step 2: Find the *y*–coordinate. Start at 0 and count to the line point *A* is on. Point *A* is 4 lines above 0. Point *A* has a *y*-coordinate of 4.

So, the coordinates for point *A* are (2, 4).

For Finding Point B

Step 1: Find the *x*–coordinate. Start at 0 and count over left to the line point *B* is on. Point *B* is 1 line to the left of 0. So, point *B* has an *x*-coordinate of -1.

Step 2: Find the *y*–coordinate. Start at 0 and count up to the line point *B* is on. Point *B* is 5 lines above 0. Point *B* has a *y*–coordinate of 5.

So, the coordinates for point *B* are (-1, 5).

Directions: Find the coordinates for the points on the graph.

1. Point A = (,   )

2. Point B = (,   )

3. Point C = (,   )

4. Point D = (,   )

5. Point E = (,   )

6. Point F = (,   )

7. Point G = (,   )

8. Point H = (,   )

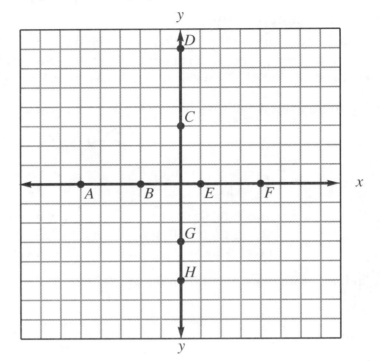

Directions: Find the coordinates for the points on the graph.

9. Point A = (,   )

10. Point B = (,   )

11. Point C = (,   )

12. Point D = (,   )

13. Point E = (,   )

14. Point F = (,   )

15. Point G = (,   )

16. Point H = (,   )

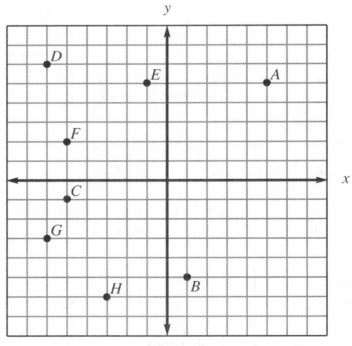

Facts to Know

A *solution* makes an equation true. The equation $x + y = 5$ has many solutions, not just one.

- If $x = 2$, then $y = 3$ since $2 + 3 = 5$.
- If $x = 0$, then $y = 5$ since $0 + 5 = 5$.
- If $x = -2$, then $y = 7$ since $-2 + 7 = 5$.

Plotting Points

For any value of x we choose in the equation $x + y = 5$, we can find a value for y that will make the statement true. If you plot the coordinates of the solutions to the equation on a graph—(2, 3), (0, 5), (-2, 7)—notice that they are in a straight line. Any point that is on this line is a solution of the equation. This line is called the graph of the equation.

Example: Graph $2x - y = 1$.

This equation has many possible solutions.

- If $x = 2$, then $y = 3$ since $4 - 3 = 1$
- If $x = 1$, then $y = 1$ since $2 - 1 = 1$
- If $x = 0$, then $y = -1$ since $0 - (-1) = 1$

Make a table of the values for x and y. Three points are enough to graph the solutions.

x	y
2	3
1	1
0	-1

The table shows the possible coordinates for the points on the graph as: (2, 3), (1, 1), (0, -1).

Now plot those points on the graph and connect the points with a line.

Any point on this line—not only the plotted points—is a solution to the equation $2x - y = 1$.

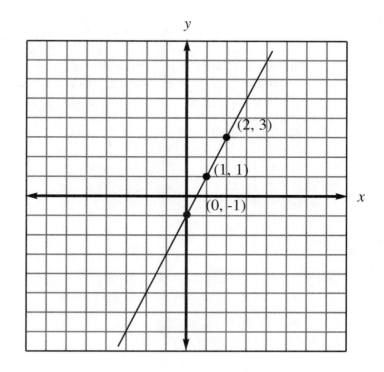

Graphing Equations

Always plot three points when you plot an equation, because although two points will make a straight line, a third point makes certain that your solution is correct. If you cannot align at least three points to form a straight line, you will know one or more of your solutions are wrong.

Example: Graph $y = 3x - 2$.

Step 1: Find three possible solutions to the equation.

Step 2: Make a chart of the possible solutions.

> If $x = 2$, $y = 3(2) - 2$
> $y = 6 - 2$
> $y = 4$

> If $x = 3$, $y = 3(3) - 2$
> $y = 9 - 2$
> $y = 7$

> If $x = 4$, $y = 3(4) - 2$
> $y = 12 - 2$
> $y = 10$

x	y
2	4
3	7
4	10

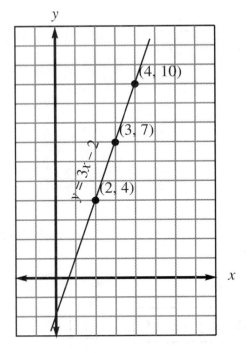

Step 3: Plot these points on a graph: (2, 4), (3, 7), (4, 10). Draw a line that connects the three points. (You can move both axes off center to gain more number places on them; see below.)

Example: $y = 2x - 3$

Step 1: Find three possible solutions to the equation.

> If $x = 5$, then $y = 7$ since $2(5) - 3 = 7$.
> If $x = 0$, then $y = -3$ since $2(0) - 3 = -3$.
> If $x = -1$, then $y = -5$ since $2(-1) - 3 = -5$.

Step 2: Make a chart of possible solutions.

x	y
5	7
0	-3
-1	-5

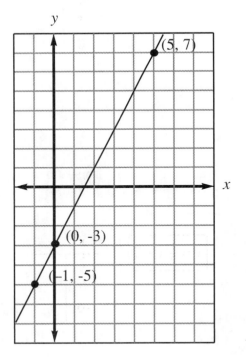

Step 3: Plot these points on a graph: (5, 7), (0, -3), (-1, -5). Draw a line connecting the points.

Directions: Graph the possible solutions for the equations.

1. $y = 2x - 8$

x	y
2	
4	
6	

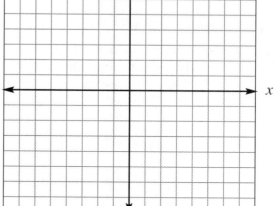

2. $y = x - 3$

x	y
-2	
5	
0	

3. $y = \frac{1}{2}x + 1$

x	y
2	
6	
-6	

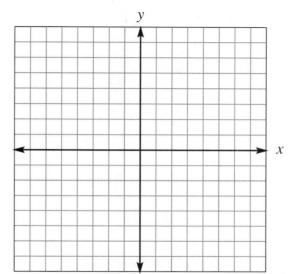

Facts to Know

Two equations can be solved by graphing both equations on the same grid. All of the points common to both graphs are solutions of the pair of equations.

Graphs and Solutions

If the two lines cross (intersect) at one point, then they have that *one* solution in common.

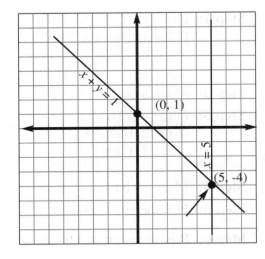

If the lines overlap (one line on top of another) the equations have *all* solutions in common.

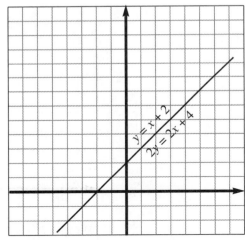

If the lines are parallel—the lines never intersect—then they have *no* solutions in common.

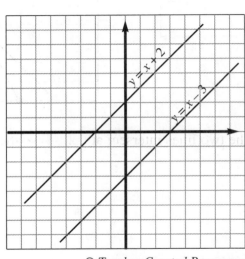

Facts to Know *(cont.)*

Graphs and Solutions *(cont.)*

Example: Graph the solutions of these two equations: $y = x - 2$ and $y = 2x$.

Step 1: Find possible solutions for the first equation: $y = x - 2$.
If $x = 1$, then $y = 1 - 2$, so $y = -1$.
If $x = 3$, then $y = 3 - 2$, so $y = 1$.
If $x = 5$, then $y = 5 - 2$, so $y = 3$.

x	y
1	-1
3	1
5	3

Step 2: Make a chart of those solutions.

Step 3: Find possible solutions for the second equation: $y = 2x$.
If $x = 2$, then $y = 2(2)$, so $y = 4$.
If $x = 4$, then $y = 2(4)$, so $y = 8$.
If $x = -4$, $y = 2(-4)$, so $y = -8$.

x	y
2	4
4	8
-4	-8

Step 4: Make a chart of the possible solutions.

Step 5: Plot the solutions to the first equation on the graph.

Step 6: Plot the solutions to the second equation on the graph.

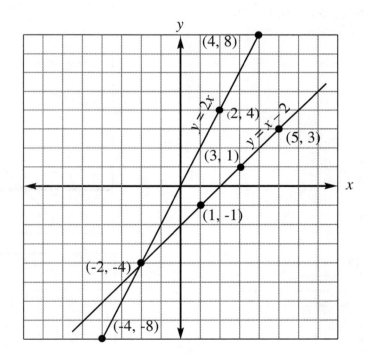

The two lines intersect at (-2, -4) so the solution is (-2, -4).

Directions: Graph the solutions to both equations.

1. $3x - 5 = y$
   $x - 5 = y$

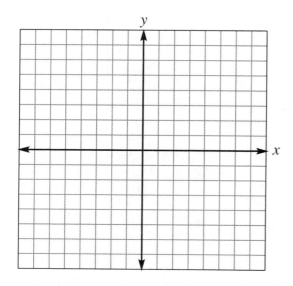

2. $2x = y$
   $4x = 2y$

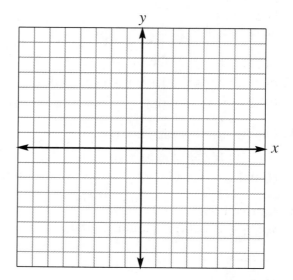

3. $y = x + 2$
   $y = x + 4$

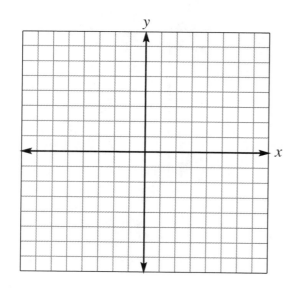

4. $y = 2x + 3$
   $y = \frac{1}{2}x$

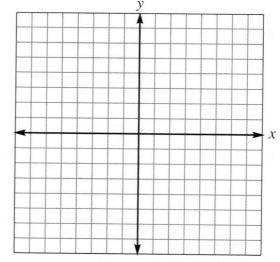

Directions: Solve these pre-algebra problems.

1. A plane for Smith Messenger Service flew the 3,200 miles from Chicago's O'Hare Airport to Los Angeles International in 5 hours. How fast was the plane flying? (Use the formula $d = rt$ or *distance = rate x time.*) _____

2. Mr. Andrews rides his bike to work in Homewood every day. His office is 10 miles from his house in Frankfort. The ride from home to work takes half an hour. How many miles per hour does he ride? (Use the formula $d = rt$ or *distance = rate x time.*) _____

3. In Mrs. Washington's keyboarding class, students must learn to type 35 words per minute. At that rate, how many words can be typed in 32 minutes? (Use the formula $w = rt$. The letter r stands for words per minute.) _____

4. On the last day of school before winter vacation, the temperature dropped to 20° Celsius. What was the temperature in degrees Fahrenheit? Use the formula $F = \frac{9}{5}(C + 32)$ or Fahrenheit $= \frac{9}{5}$ x (Celsius + 32). _____

5. Latrice bought a CD player on sale for $60. That was 25% off ($\frac{1}{4}$ less than the regular price). What was the regular price? (*Hint:* Let x = the regular price. Don't take 25% of $60!). _____

6. Holly, Heidi, Lauren, and Andrew spent a total of $16 at Cal's fast food drive-in. Each one bought a veggie burger and fries. A burger costs a dollar more than an order of french fries.

   (*Hint:* Let x = price of french fries. Then $x + \$1$ = price of a burger.)

   (a) How much does a burger cost? _____

   (b) How much does an order of french fries cost? _____

7. At James Hart Middle School there are 561 students in grades 6–8. The number of girls is 15 more than twice the number of boys. _____

   (*Hint:* Let x = the number of boys. Then $2x + 15$ = the number of girls.) _____

   (a) How many girls are there? _____

   (b) How many boys? _____

8. US Messenger Service has to make a delivery from Chicago to Carbondale, Illinois. Dave drove 200 miles in 5 hours. If he kept driving at the same rate, how far would he go in 8 hours? (*Hint:* Set up a proportion. Use x for the missing term $\frac{200 \text{ miles}}{5 \text{ hours}} = \frac{x \text{ miles}}{8 \text{ hours}}$.) _____

9. Tiffany stands next to a tree. She is 5 feet tall and casts a shadow $2\frac{1}{2}$ feet long. The tree casts a shadow 8 feet long. How tall is the tree? (*Hint:* Set up a proportion as in #8.) _____

10. Dave drove 90 miles to Porter, Indiana, in $1\frac{1}{2}$ hours. How long will it take to drive 300 miles? (*Hint:* See #8.) _____

11. Mr. Wilson has been looking everywhere for the official survey of his property. Finally when he finds it, half the paper has been water damaged. The property lines have faded. All he can figure out is that the perimeter of his lot is 308 feet. The length is 25 feet more than twice the width. What are the length and width of Mr. Wilson's lot? length _____ width _____

12. Manny, Gabriella, and Ingrid went into business selling candles at Halloween. Manny invested twice as much as Gabriella. Ingrid invested $500 more than Gabriella. How should a profit of $2,200 be divided? Gabriella _____ Manny _____ Ingrid _____

13. The Rich East High School little theater holds 220 people. Adult tickets for *Romeo & Juliet* are $1.50. Students discount tickets are $0.80. On Friday night, the auditorium was full and the total from ticket sales was $274. How many adults attended the play? _____

14. Eli is a bricklayer. The second day he laid bricks twice the length of the first day. For the next ten days, he laid brick at the same rate as the second day and completed the 100-foot wall. How many feet did he lay the first day? _____

15. Todd is building a bookcase. Below are the dimensions of the finished bookcase. Write and solve an equation for the missing distances between the shelves. Each of the four boards used as shelves and as the top and base are 1 inch thick. _____

    a. How tall is the top shelf?

    _____

    b. How tall is the middle shelf?

    _____

    c. How tall is the lower shelf?

    _____

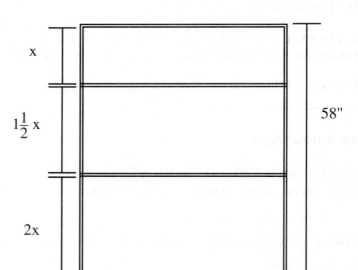

Directions: Solve these challenging brain teasers.

1. Tony saved d dollars in January. In February, he saved $5 more than he saved in January.

   (a) Write an expression that represents the number of dollars he saved in February.

   _____

   (b) Write an expression that represents the total number of dollars he saved in two months.

   _____

2. The length of a rectangle is four feet more than the width. Let w be the number of feet in the width. Then $(w + 4)$ is the number of feet in the length. Write equations for the following:

   (a) The width when doubled is the same as the length increased by three. _____

   (b) Assume the length doubled is equal to the product of 3 and the width increased by 1.

   _____

   (c) Twice the width added to twice the length is equal to 36. (This is the perimeter of the rectangle.) _____

3. In shop class, Don cut a 50-inch board into two pieces. One piece is 10 inches longer than the other piece. Find the length of the shorter piece. _____

4. In a class election, Ian received 5 more votes than Libbie. How many votes did Ian receive if all 35 students in the class voted? _____

5. If a number is added to twice the same number, the sum is less than 27. For what numbers greater than zero is this true? _____

6. The sum of three consecutive whole numbers is 123. What are the three numbers?

   _____

Riddles About Age

7. Mr. O'Leary is 4 times as old as his son. In 16 years he will be only twice as old. What are their ages. (*Hint:* If the son is x years old now, how old will he be in another 16 years?)

   _____

8. Mary is 14 years old. She is five years older than her brother. How old is Mary's brother?

   _____

9. A boy is four years younger than his sister. If the boy is 10 years old, how old is his sister?

   _____

10. A boy's age seven years from now will be 20. How old is the boy now? _____

11. Anne was 3 years old ten years ago. How old is Anne at the present time? _____

12. If one is added to twice a girl's age, the result is 19. What is the girl's age? _____

Try These If You Dare!

13. Gloria had $40.00 in savings. Her mother gave her another $30.00 and her grandmother gave her $10.00 to buy a pair of running shoes. The pair of running shoes Gloria wants cost $54.99, tax included. Write an equation using a variable to describe the amount of money that Gloria will have to contribute from her savings to buy the shoes. _____

14. Uncle Henry grew 252 kilograms of cherries. He sold them to a grocer who divided them into 5-kg and 2-kg bags. If the grocer uses the same number of 5-kg bags as 2-kg bags, then how many bags did the grocer use in all? _____

15. An 800-seat multiplex is divided into 3 theatres. There are 270 seats in Theatre 1, and there are 150 more seats in Theatre 2 than in Theatre 3. How many seats are in Theatre 2? (*Hint:* Let x = number of seats in Theatre 3; T1 = Theatre 1 = 270 seats T2 = Theatre 2 = $150 + x$; T1 + T2 + T3 = 800 seats) _____

16. The sum of 13 and twice a number is 75. Find the number. _____

17. Manuel has a board 16 feet long. He needs to cut it so that one piece is 1 foot longer than twice the length of the other. (*Hint:* If x = the length of the short board, then $2x + 1$ = the length of the longer board.) What will be the length of each board? _____

18. The sum of three consecutive integers is 69. What are the numbers? (*Hint:* Let x = the smallest number, $x + 1$ = the next smallest number, and $(x + 1) + 1$ or $x + 2$ = the third number). _____

19. April wants her house to be a pale yellow. Pale yellow paint is made by mixing paint in a ratio of 9 parts white to 2 parts yellow. How much of each color is needed to make 22 gallons of pale yellow paint? _____

20. Margo sells perfume at the Smith and Jones department store. She makes $8.00 an hour and 15% commission on any bottle of perfume she sells. If each bottle of perfume costs $50 and she earned $ 470 in 5 days, how many bottles of perfume did she sell? _____

Directions: Solve each system of equations below and on page 44 by graphing them. Using the solution, find the letter in the chart on page 44 which matches the solution for each problem. Write this letter on the blank space which is labeled with the problem number. The resulting message will be the answer to the riddle.

1. $y = 3x$
   $y = \frac{1}{3}x$
   (,)
   solution

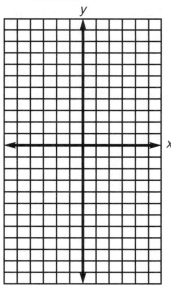

2. $x = -5$
   $y = x + -3$
   (,)
   solution

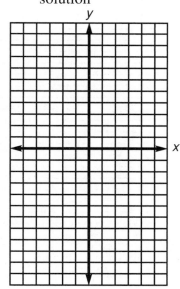

3. $y = -x$
   $y = 3x + 4$
   (,)
   solution

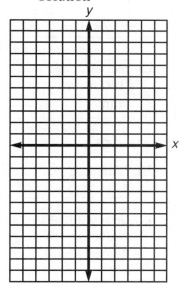

4. $y = x + 4$
   $y = 2x + 5$
   (,)
   solution

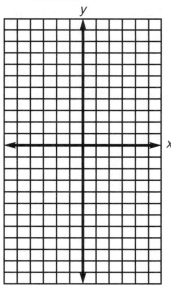

5. $y = 2x$
   $y = 3x - 3$
   (,)
   solution

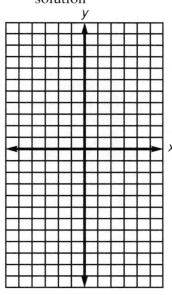

6. $x = 4$
   $y = -2$
   (,)
   solution

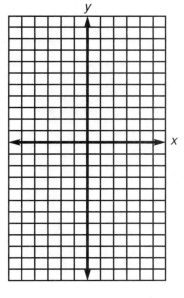

7. $y = 4 + 2x$
   $y - x = 4$
   (,   )
   solution

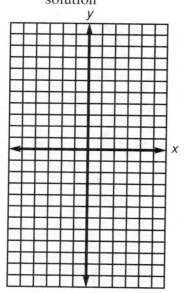

8. $y = 5x$
   $y = x + 4$
   (,   )
   solution

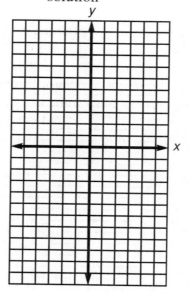

9. $y - 2x = 3$
   $y = x + 3$
   (,   )
   solution

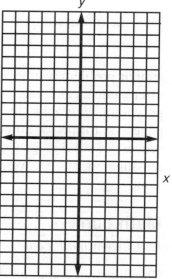

10. $y - 2x = 1$
    $y - x = -1$
    (,   )
    solution

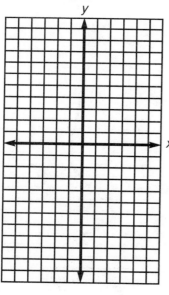

A (-1, -5)	**N** (-1, 3)
B (0, 3)	**O** (8, 4)
C (1, 5)	**P** (3, 9)
D (-1, 1)	**R** (-1, 6)
E (-3, -2)	**S** (3, 6)
F (10, 6)	**T** (1, 2)
G (-5, -8)	**U** (0, 4)
H (5, 10)	**V** (4, -2)
I (0, 0)	**W** (6, 1)
L (9, 4)	**Y** (-2, -3)
M (-4, -9)	

Question: What is it called when a cartoon dog plunges into the water?

___ ___ ___ ___ ___
 5   8   7   9   10

___ ___ ___ ___ ___ ___
 3   1   6   1   4   2

Directions: Here are some Internet sites which help explain pre-algebra and algebra concepts and offers homework help too. **Note:** Teachers and parents can check these sites in advance so they can ascertain whether they are age and topic appropriate for children.

Algebra.com

http://www.algebra.com

This site offers straightforward methods of solving algebraic equations with word problem examples and applied formulas. It even has an option to "customize" a sample word problem to find the solution for a similar problem, using new variables. The many calculator "solvers" offer students an instant evaluation of linear and quadratic equations, polynomials, graphs, and more, along with optional related practice pages. A forum for homework help assists with questions about the process of solving a specific equation posted by the student on a message board. Answered personally, responses are usually posted the same day.

Math.com

http://www.math.com

The directory found on this site's homepage provides its own search engine and opens to a section for students that offers free learning and homework assistance. The full listing of algebra lessons, organized by subject, contains quizzes, test preparations, and study-tip pages. Additional resources include games, references, and links to tutorial products, as well as one-on-one online tutorial sessions to provide more in-depth lessons. In the event any review or extension exercises are needed, pre-algebra and geometry lessons are also available on this site.

Math—Algebra

http://library.thinkquest.org/10030/algecon.htm

Organized like a table of contents, the site is an extensive directory of examples and lessons divided into sections progressively, similar to chapters of a book. Using the step-by-step approaches to evaluating equations demonstrated, this textbook-like resource supplements the learning that takes place in the classroom. The thoroughly explained and simply delivered information covers concepts such as number systems, equations and equality, functions, graphing (of varying difficulty), and linear, as well as discrete, algebra.

Page 8
1. -2
2. 3
3. -4
4. -9
5. 9
6. -110
7. -43
8. 2.7
9. 23
10. 7.89
11. -6
12. 4
13. -13
14. 15
15. -6
16. 12
17. 50
18. 12
19. 4
20. 7
21. -7
22. 4.4
23. -4.4
24. 18
25. 12
26. 17
27. -9
28. 16
29. -10
30. 7
31. 24
32. 5
33. -19
34. 15

Page 12
1. 63
2. 68.2
3. 46.2

4. 100
5. 54
6. 924
7. 60
8. -24
9. -70
10. -36
11. 24
12. -90
13. -4
14. -5
15. -3
16. 11
17. 3
18. 9
19. 3
20. 1
21. 3
22. 7
23. -2
24. 3
25. -27
26. 54
27. 28
28. -65
29. -13
30. 35
31. 2/9
32. -5
33. 4
34. -5

Pages 15 and 16
1. $14/x$
2. $7x$
3. $x - 10$
4. $x + 12$
5. $x + y$ or $y + x$
6. $x/6$
7. $4x + 5x$

8. $4x + 5y$
9. $x/3 + 7$ or $1/3x + 7$
10. $25/x$
11. $\dfrac{6 + x}{10}$
12. $1/2\,(8x)$ or $8x/2$
13. $\dfrac{5 + x}{7}$
14. $\dfrac{4 + x}{10}$
15. $20 - 4x$
16. $\dfrac{20 + x}{5}$
17. $w + 5$ or $5 + w$
18. $c/3$ or $1/3c$
19. one number added to another number
20. one number decreased by another number
21. 4 times a number
22. 8 divided by a number
23. 2 times a number, decreased by 5
24. 8 increased by a number
25. a number times another number
26. 22 decreased by a number
27. 22 less than a number
28. $4y$
29. $2b$
30. $3r$
31. $-c$
32. $1\,2/3d + 3b$
33. $12r^2 - 3s + r$
34. $x + 1$

35. $3n - 5$ or $-5 + 3n$
36. $3x + 2y^3 - 4y$
37. $-2x + 3y$
38. $\dfrac{3}{9} = \dfrac{1}{3}$
39. $3(9) = 27$
40. $3/3 + 9/3 = 12/3 = 4$
41. $3 + 9 = 12$
42. $\dfrac{9}{3} = 3$
43. $5(-4) = -20$
44. $-4 + 10 = 6$
45. $\dfrac{10}{5} = 2$
46. $10 - 5 = 5$
47. $\dfrac{-4}{10} = \dfrac{-2}{5}$

Page 20
1. 48
2. 55
3. 46
4. 112
5. -5
6. 2
7. -1 1/3 or -4/3
8. 29
9. 14
10. 5
11. 15° C
12. 135 miles
13. $280
14. 360 feet
15. $b = -12$
16. $y = 80$
17. $a = 42$
18. $t = 144$
19. $n = 35$
20. $x = -8$
21. $a = -125$
22. $c = 18$

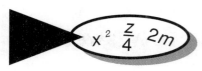

Page 24

1. $a = 8$
2. $z = 9$
3. $b = 36$
4. $w = 264$
5. $c = 16$
6. $d = 3$
7. $x = 2$
8. $x = 3$
9. $x = 1$
10. $x = 6$
11. $x = 1/2$
12. $x = 1$
13. $x = 2$
14. $y = 3/2$
15. $x = 4$
16. $x = 22$
17. $n = 3\ 1/2$ or $7/2$
18. $a = 7\ 1/3$ or $22/3$
19. $a = -2$
20. $r = 17$
21. $r = 5$
22. $y = 2$
23. $y = 5$
24. $x = 4$
25. $w = 5$
26. $b = -6$

Page 27

1. $x = 3$
2. $x = 39$
3. $b = 2$
4. $x = -1\ 1/2$ or $-3/2$
5. $x = -1$
6. $x = -16$
7. $x = 2\ 3/5$ or $13/5$
8. $x = -13$
9. $x = -5$
10. $x = 7$
11. $x = 12$

12. $x = 20$

Page 28

1. $y = b - c - d$
2. $x = \dfrac{a + b}{t}$
3. $m = \dfrac{p - w}{s}$
4. $x = r + t$
5. $x = ab$
6. $x = w - y$
7. $x = \dfrac{b}{d}$
8. $x = p - b$
9. $x = \dfrac{h}{w}$
10. $y = \dfrac{d - a}{c}$
11. $l = \dfrac{A}{w}$
12. $t = \dfrac{d}{r}$
13. $x = \dfrac{z - y}{b}$
14. $r = \dfrac{t - s}{c}$
15. $b = \dfrac{cd}{a}$
16. $s = \dfrac{tv}{r}$
17. $z = \dfrac{w - x}{y}$
18. b equals the square root of $c^2 - a^2$ or $b = \sqrt{c^2 - a^2}$
19. $r = \dfrac{C}{2\pi}$
20. $w = \dfrac{p - 2l}{2}$

Page 32

1. $(-5, 0)$
2. $(-2, 0)$
3. $(0, 3)$
4. $(0, 7)$

5. $(1, 0)$
6. $(4, 0)$
7. $(0, -3)$
8. $(0, -5)$
9. $(5, 5)$
10. $(1, -5)$
11. $(-5, -1)$
12. $(-6, 6)$
13. $(-1, 5)$
14. $(-5, 2)$
15. $(-6, -3)$
16. $(-3, -6)$

Page 35

1.

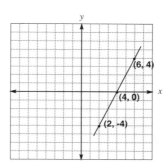

2.

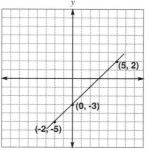

3.

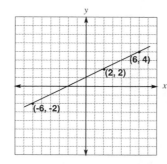

Page 38

1.

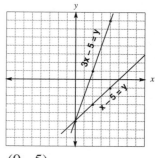

$(0, -5)$

2.

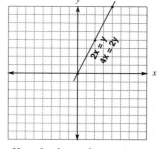

all solutions in common

3.

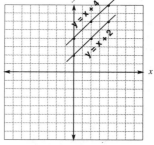

no solution

4.

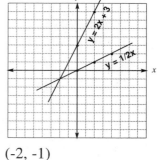

$(-2, -1)$

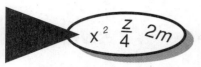

Pages 39 and 40

1. 640 mph

2. 20 mph

3. $w = 1{,}120$ words

4. $F = 93.6°$

5. $3/4x = \$60$
   $x = \$80$

6. $4x + 4$
   $(x + \$1) = \$16$
   a) $x + \$1 = \$2.50$
      for a burger
   b) $x = \$1.50$ for
      French fries

7. $x + 2x + 15 = 561$
   a) $2x + 15 = 379$
      girls
   b) $x = 182$ boys

8. $1600 = 5x$
   Dave can drive
   320 miles in 8
   hours.

9. $\dfrac{5}{2.5} = \dfrac{x}{8}$
   $x = 16$ ft.
   The tree is 16 feet
   tall.

10. $90x = 450$
    $x = 5$ hours
    Dave can drive
    300 miles in 5
    hours.

11. $2(2w + 25) + 2w = 308$
    $w = 43$ feet =
    width
    $2w + 25 = 111$
    feet = length

12. $x + 2x + x + 500$
    $= \$2{,}200$
    $x = \$425$ for
    Gabriella
    $2x = \$850$ for
    Manny
    $x + 500 = \$925$
    for Ingrid

13. $1.50x + .80(220 - x) = \$274$
    $x = 140$ adults

14. $x + 2x + 10(2x) = 100$
    $x = 4.3$ ft.

15. $1 + x + 1 + 1\,1/2x + 1 + 2x + 1 = 58$
    $x = 12"$
    $1\,1/2x = 18"$
    $2x = 24"$

Pages 41 and 42

1. a. $d + 5$
   b. $d + d + 5$ or
      $2d + 5$

2. a. $2w = (w + 4) + 3$
   b. $2(w + 4) = (3w + 1)$
   c. $2w + 2(w + 4) = 36$

3. $n + n + 10 = 50$,
   $n = 20$ inches

4. $n + 5 + n = 35$,
   $n = 15$ votes; $5 + n = 20$ votes for Ian

5. $n + 2n < 27$
   $n < 9$

6. $n + n + 1 + n + 2 = 123$
   $3n + 3 = 123$,
   $n = 40$; the
   numbers are 40,
   41, and 42.

7. Father = 32 years,
   son = 8 years

8. $n + 5 = 14$,
   $n = 9$ years old

9. $n - 4 = 10$,
   $n = 14$ years old

10. $x + 7 = 20$,
    $x = 13$ years old

11. $x - 10 = 3$,
    $x = 13$ years old

12. $1 + 2n = 19$,
    $n = 9$ years old

13. Let x = Gloria's
    contribution
    $\$30.00 + \$10.00 = \$40.00$
    $\$40.00 + x = \$54.99$
    $x = \$14.99$

14. Let x = total
    number of bags
    $5(1/2\,x) + 2(1/2\,x) = 252$
    $2.5x + 1x = 252$
    $3.5x = 252$
    $x = 72$ bags

15. $270 + (150 + x) + x = 800$
    $420 + 2x = 800$
    $x = 190$ seats
    If there are $x = 190$ seats in
    Theatre 3, then
    Theatre 2 has
    $150 + 190 = 340$
    seats

16. $2n + 13 = 75$
    Add (-13) to both
    sides.
    $2n = 62$
    Divide both sides
    by 2.
    $n = 31$

17. $x + (2x + 1) = 16$
    $x = 5'$
    $2x + 1 = 11'$

18. $x + (x + 1) + (x + 2) = 69$
    $x = 22$
    $x + 1 = 23$
    $x + 2 = 24$

19. $9x + 2x = 22$
    4 gallons yellow
    18 gallons white

20.

$(\$8 \times 40) + .15(\$50x) =$	$\$470$
$\$320 + \$7.5x =$	$\$470$
$- \$320$	$= -\$320$
$\$7.5x =$	$\$150$
$\$7.5 =$	$\$7.5$
$x =$	20

Pages 43 and 44

Scuby Diving